THE HUMAN CUSTOMER EXPERIENCE

AND THE NOT-SO-SECRET FORMULA

THE HUMAN CUSTOMER EXPERIENCE

AND THE NOT-SO-SECRET FORMULA

D. M. Palmer

If you enjoyed this book please leave a review on Amazon, Good Reads, Google, or you preferred book review platform. Your review helps ensure others find this book as well. For indie authors, you are our only way of life! Thank you so much for your support!
This QR code will take you directly to Amazon to review this book.

Please go to DesireeMPalmer.com to check out Desiree's other work. To sign up for her newsletter go to Satori.pub
When you sign up, you will receive free downloadable PDF worksheet based on this publication to use with your business. Just say which publication you purchased when signing up!
This QR code will take you directly to Satori.Pub to sign up for the newsletter and request your PDF.

The Human Customer Experience and the Not-So-Secret Formula.

ISBN 978-1499611397

Copyright © 2014 Desiree M. Palmer and Satori, LLC doing business as Satori Publishing

Dedication

To all the hustlers, side giggers, ma and papers, and get-er-done'ers.

This is for us!

I know it is hard. I am in the trenches with you. I know you just want to do the right thing. I know you don't have time or money or waste.

Just remember, you already have everything you need to create the best experience possible for your customers.

Get strategic. Take some time out, map out the perfect journey. Put a few strategies in place. Where will you get the most bang for your buck. Where can you create the biggest connections with the least effort and expense? That is where you start.

TABLE OF CONTENTS

INTRODUCTION

An irritating screeching noise, inches from your head, wakes you up. Reminding you, in an all too familiar way, it's time to start another work week. You pause few moments before your eyes open and think back to Friday when you bought Powerball tickets.

Why couldn't you have gotten the winning numbers? You wonder. Oh, wait.

You just remembered.

It's Monday!

Recently, Monday has become your new favorite day of the week.

A few months ago, you started dating a new person. After searching longer than you would have liked, with very little luck, you finally felt like you found exactly what you have been looking for. Everything has been going well. Of course, like every relationship, there has been some growing pains, a hiccup here or there, but things were pretty easy to work out. The best part, well, one of them anyway, every Monday, without fail, they send you a little gift. It isn't much, maybe chocolates, flowers, have a coffee delivered or your favorite meal at lunch. Something that lets you know this relationship is important. It really makes you appreciate them and what they have to offer. Not the gift as much as the gesture. It's thoughtful and you feel valued.

You think to yourself. I can do this again after all. I have my little treat to look forward to! So, you get up get on your way and head off to work.

You wait all day. But, nothing shows up. You wonder if maybe it's coming this evening instead. It's been like clockwork, there is no way they forgot.

The Human Customer Experience

The evening rolls around, they call to say hi and see how your day was, you make small talk, and nothing else is said. They don't even mention anything. This is odd you think to yourself. Still, a missed gift is nothing to fret over. You make a couple excuses and move on certain the next week the lovely gesture will resume.

Over the next week your relationship is completely normal in every way, the same dates, the same calls, the same silly text messages and good night emoji. There is no sign anything has changed. You are reassured their feelings haven't changed.

It's Monday again. This time you are a little hesitant but mostly certain. Afterall, you two have an amazing relationship, equally giving and receiving. Why would this gesture stop. Only, by the end of this second Monday, there is still no little surprise.

Now you are worried. Twice in a row. Did something change? Did their feelings change? Did you do something to make them pull back a bit? Should you be worried something more is happening?

If you are being 100 percent honest, you do resent the changed behavior a bit. It wasn't as much about the gift as it was about showing you they cared. They appreciated you. Now, what, they just don't anymore.

There is no sense in letting this wonder and worry just continue. You decide to call and ask.

"So, I noticed, these last couple Monday's you haven't send anything to let me know you were thinking of me. I have really appreciated when you did that. Has something happened to make this stop?"

With a rather matter fact tone, they simply reply, as if the single statement is everything you need to understand.

"The Monday gift portion of our relationship has ended. That was just a promotion to entice you to get to know me and try out dating me. Now that we are more inclined to keep dating, there will be no more Monday gifts."

Ummm, What?!?

Who does that? Is this really the relationship you signed up for? Did you miss the fine print? Since when did relationships have fine print?

Here you thought you bought a book on business. So why is it starting with a story on dating? Hang tight, it will all make sense.

You have heard, "It's not personal, it's just business." While that might be true in a business to business transaction, and I would argue that it still is only on shaky ground at best in those cases, anytime there is a human on the other side of the interaction, your transaction, your relationship, is personal.

Humans aren't wired to consider a transaction where there is money involved with different emotions than where there isn't money involved. If we were, then when we lend money to friends or family, we should naturally become disassociated to the transaction. Afterall, it's just business right. Money doesn't change a relationship and make it impersonal.

A business transaction, a friendship, a relationship, a long standing business partnership, all these relationships work and act just like a human personal relationship. That is a good thing. Because we have been studying the human relationship for centuries. We have a lot of data to help us understand how to build the perfect customer interaction.

The truth is the way we feel in a personal relationship is a natural and intuitive process. Humans are wired with emotions that naturally react. These same "wires" snap and fire in all our relationships. Dr. Paul MacLean first theorized the Triune or "lizard" brain in the 1950s; it's a place in our brain that works on autopilot in times of trouble or pain without thinking. It makes us spring into action when we need to fight or flee. There are pathways for emotions guiding our lives and our relationships. They tell us when we are hurt, when we are happy, and how to react. These pathways let us know in a relationship when to jump in with both feet or wait on the shore until a better catch comes along.

No more than the "lizard" knows the difference between a scary dream that makes your heart race, your "Juliet" doesn't know if her Romeo is a suitor, a stranger, or a business. Your emotions become involved in every relationship in life.

Why do you cry at the end of a romantic comedy? Because even if your head knows that Gerard Butler doesn't die in P.S. I Love You, your emotions don't. They engage and before you know it you are ugly crying into a pile of tissues and eating a pint of Ice Cream.

As a business, if you offer your customer a discount on a product of service for a period of time then stop, you're committing a cardinal relationship sin. To the customer, you're one long "We have to talk..." pause away from an awkward conversation. The value of the relationship is changed. You didn't even give them a chance to talk about it. Your customer goes into fight or, more likely, flight mode. Doing this as way to encourage them to buy isn't going to get the long term relationship you are hoping for. They will stick around for the discount, and some might hang on a little longer. But eventually, they will jump to the next offer. You want to earn the relationship because you are the best deal in town. Not because you are the cheapest date.

Customer Experience experts would like you to believe it's hard to figure out how to get, keep, and grow your customer base. In fact, my career relies on it. When I was in the corporate world my job was to interpret customer data (known as Voice of the Customer or VOC) and make improvement recommendations to senior executives. This "not-so-secret formula" I am going to share with you guided my decisions when designing the customer experience.

The Human Customer Experience

My philosophy is, when you do what is right for the customer the bottom line always pays you back.

In truth, customer relationships are one of the easiest things in the world to understand if you can grasp the singularly true concept that, it isn't JUST business, it is VERY personal. Every interaction is personal for the customer, anyway.

I discovered by understand the three concepts I will teach you in this book I was able

THE THREE MODELS

(Table 1.1)

Three concepts make up the substance of this theory: the **Duration and Choice Model**, the **Relationship Correlation Model**, and an adaptation of Maslow's hierarchy of human needs called **Customer's Hierarchy of Needs**.

The first concept—**Duration and Choice Model**—details how in every relationship there is a certain amount of choice and an estimated time frame of existence. Some relationships, like those between a parent and child, have little to no choice, while others, such as marriage, are typically all choice. Relationships also have a finite timeframe. Some will only be in passing – you meet a fun person at a party and never see them again. Then you have longer term relationships like those with a spouse or a best friend. Business relationships have the same indicators, a finite duration, and some amount of choice. In other words, some industries are designed for longer relationships like grocery stores, while others may only ever be a single purchase, like when buying a home.

The second concept—**Relationship Correlation Model**—takes the traditional relationship cycle: attraction, courtship, commitment, etc. and correlates that to business relationships. Attraction relates to marketing as commitment relates to purchase and so on. There are classic ways we humans tend to screw up the difference phases of relationships or, conversely, how we can make a positive difference.

The final concept—**Customer's Hierarchy of Needs**—is adapted from Maslow's Hierarchy of Needs model. Maslow explained that there are five levels of basic human needs a person strives to meet in his life. Each level is dependent on achieving the one before it. As an example, you must first have shelter, food, and safety, before you can worry about learning a trade or skill. With customer relationships, you have the same levels of needs, basic steps that must be reached before you can move on. It will not do any good to show customers you appreciate their business if your product or service doesn't work.

There are plenty of resources that talk about the science behind why it matters to have great customer relationships. There are resources on how to measure for it, how to recognize it and how to strategize for it. However, there aren't many resources that help the reader fully engage their own intuitive nature; none that "teach you to fish." This theory builds upon the groundwork laid by the earlier studies and takes it to the next step. The Human Customer Experience (HCE) theory removes the sterile scientific nature from the equation, allowing you to understand the principles so you can successfully and intuitively apply them to your customers today.

You already know what makes great customer relationships; through experience in personal relationships. A Business relationship has to respect the bond and honor the 'human' inside the customer. It isn't rocket science; but it isn't easy either. If you were to ask any married person what the single most difficult relationship in their life is, odds are it will be with their spouse. Nonetheless, it is also the most rewarding, especially when done well.

The Human Customer Experience

UNDERSTANDING RELATIONSHIPS

PERSONAL RELATIONSHIP MODELS

Relationships, long lasting ones, are expensive. We invest in different ways; our time, money, and our emotions. You can figure out the type of relationship you have by using the **Duration and Choice Model** (DCM). This model is the basic foundation for every customer type. Another important factor is where you are in the relationship cycle, the model used here best aligns to the Enduring relationship, one that has choice and is long lasting. This model is called the **Relationship Correlation Model** (RCM). You must understand which part of the relationship you are in to understand what kind of investment is needed.

RELATIONSHIP TYPES

DCM – There are four main relationship types that all relationships fall into. This is diagrammed in a quadrant model using the anagram T.I.M.E. The two axes are duration and choice, ranging from high to low. T.I.M.E. stands for: **T**olerable, **I**nsignificant, **M**emorable, and **E**nduring. Depending on where your industry falls in the DCM you will know how much of an investment should be made to keep the relationship.

(Table 1.2)

The Human Customer Experience

RELATIONSHIP CYCLE

This is built from a basic cycle for personal relationships. The model includes seven phases:

- Attraction,
- Courtship,
- Commitment,
- Trial and Error,
- Make It Right,
- Fork in the Road, and
- Recommit or Separate.

Another piece to the

PERSONAL RELATIONSHIP CYCLE

OTHER SUITORS

RECOMMITMENT

FORK IN THE ROAD

MAKE IT RIGHT

TRIAL & ERROR

COMMITMENT

COURTSHIP

ATTRACTION

SEPERATION

puzzle is other suitors; while not a phase it is something which you must always be aware.

The full cycle is most closely aligned to the customer type "Enduring." Each customer type has its own cycle and therefore should be considered with its proper cycle. (Table 1.3)

INVESTMENT

Investments are made in three ways: Time, Emotion, and Money. Relationships that have a shorter duration and little choice do not require as much investment. Likewise, relationships where there are a lot of options and will be long lasting require more commitment and investment to ensure it endures.

(Table 1.4)

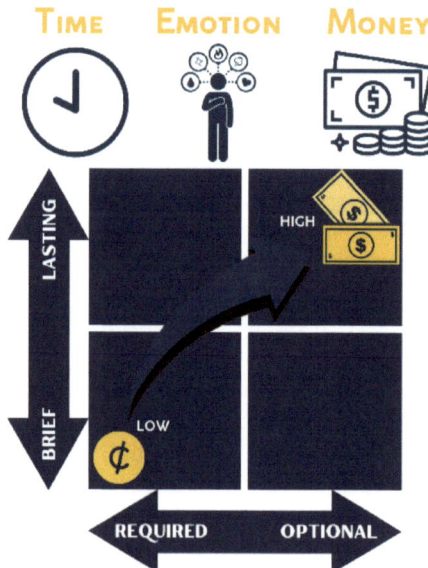

INVESTMENT

TIME   EMOTION   MONEY

LASTING

BRIEF

HIGH

LOW

REQUIRED   OPTIONAL

APPLYING THE RELATIONSHIP MODELS

DURATION AND CHOICE MODEL:

Once you understand the type of relationship your industry or business naturally has with its customers and your know what phase you are in with each touch point you start to discover the emotions involved and build better processes. New customers have a different expectation and reaction than long term customers, or even customers who have been with you for a short while. A strong customer life cycle plan will include planning for each of the phases and the customers that align with your type of customer relationship. To begin this discovery, we will discuss the DCM model and each quadrant. As you go through this be think about what area you feel your business falls within. There will be an exercise to help you find this after this section.

RELATIONSHIP TYPES: UNDERSTANDING INVESTMENT

TOLERABLE- Low choice with high duration.

Tolerable relationships are similar to what you have with an in-law. You are not given much choice and the relationship will carry on throughout your life. You must invest, even though you have no guarantee on return. You still must support a minimum standard. These relationships can be good or bad; however, they exist either way. In business, this can be compared to the electric company. On the DCM, this falls in the upper left quadrant.

INSIGNIFICANT- Low choice with low duration.

Insignificant relationships are similar to what you have with the person standing behind you in line at the grocery store. You don't have a choice in who it is, and the relationship is brief. You do not invest in this relationship, and none is needed. In business, it is similar to a toll booth. If you need to use the highway, you have to use the toll booth— there aren't options. Here again the interaction is brief. On the DCM, this falls in the lower left quadrant.

MEMORABLE- High choice with low duration.

Memorable relationships are similar to those you have with a childhood friend or a brief romantic encounter. Just like in personal relationships, these can be memorable in a good way, or in a bad way. In business, it is similar to your real-estate agent or your new car salesman. This transaction is for a large purchase and/or only a few times throughout your life. These are the relationships in which you both freely and willingly invest. You are excited to buy a home and they are excited to earn a commission. There is mutual benefit and typically these are short lived. These are also relationships that are likely to carry strong emotions. On the DCM, this is in the lower right quadrant.

ENDURING- High choice and high duration.

Enduring relationships are the biggest relationships in your life, those with a spouse or lifelong friend. In business, think of someplace you always go: the grocery store, your bank, your insurance agent or even your mortgage company. This is the business that shows up most often and with the highest dollars spent on your monthly budget These are the relationships that your both freely invest in knowing that you are fostering a long term relationship. Failure to invest will cause the relationship to fall apart. On the DCM, this is the upper right quadrant. This is the type that most closely aligns to the traditional relationship cycle described in the RCM.

On the following pages are decision questions to help you learn where your company aligns on the chart. The sample company is a cable provider whose answers are highlighted in light blue.

As discussed on the copywrite page, if you would like printable worksheets to complete these exercises, just scan the QR code on that page and follow the instructions.

The Human Customer Experience

First, we find the Duration scale.

DURATION AND CHOICE MODEL
DETERMINING YOUR POSITION ON THE DURATION SCALE

CONSIDER YOUR TYPICAL CUSTOMER WHEN ANSWERING.

HOW OFTEN DOES YOUR CUSTOMER GIVE YOU MONEY? (REOCCURRING FEEDS)

| ONCE | <5 TIMES | YEARLY | MONTHLY | WEEKLY | DAILY |

HOW OFTEN DOES YOUR CUSTOMER MAKE AN ADDITIONAL PURCHASE?

| ONCE | <5 TIMES | YEARLY | MONTHLY | WEEKLY | DAILY |

WHAT IS A REALISTIC EXPECTATION FOR A NEW PURCHASE?

| ONCE | <5 TIMES | YEARLY | MONTHLY | WEEKLY | DAILY |

WHAT IS THE AVERAGE CUSTOMER LIFE SPAN? (HOW LONG DO YOU MEASURE LIFE TIME VALUE)

| I DAY | <3 MONTHS | <I YEAR | 1-2 YRS | 2-9 YRS | 10+ YRS |
| 1 | 2 | 3 | 4 | 5 | 6 |

BRIEF   X   LASTING

SUM YOUR ANSWERS: __18__ DIVIDE BY 4: __4.5__

THIS IS YOUR POSITION ON THE DURATION SCALE.

Example: In blue above is an example of a Cable providers answer.
4,4,4,6 = 18
18/4= **4.5** (position marked on scale above with an X)

Second, we find the Choice scale.

DURATION AND CHOICE MODEL
DETERMINING YOUR POSITION ON THE CHOICE SCALE

CONSIDER YOUR TYPICAL CUSTOMER WHEN ANSWERING.

Is your product or service a want or need? (Think food v. Jewelry)

| NEED | MORE OF A NEED | MORE OF A WANT | WANT |

How many people have your use what you are selling?

| ALL | MOST | SEVERAL | SOME | FEW | RARE |

How many competitors are within your typical shoppers path?

| RARE | FEW | SOME | MORE | SEVERAL | ABUNDANT |

Are there other options for fulfilling their desire for your product or service?

| NO | NOT EXACTLY THE SAME | CLOSE TO SAME | YES |
| 1 | 2 | 3 | 4 | 5 | 6 |

REQUIRED   **X OPTIONAL**

Sum your answers: 18 Divide by 4: 4.5

This is your position on the Duration Scale.

Example: In blue above is an example of a Cable Providers answer.
6, 2, 4, 6 = 18
18/4=**4.5** (position marked on scale above with an X)

13

The Human Customer Experience

Using the example of "Cable Providers" and plotting their place on the DCM we see they align to an Enduring relationship. Understanding that this type of customer relationship is lasting and optional, you can then start to plan the kind of customer treatment cycle you want to develop. Because the desire for a longer relationship is two sided, Both the customer and the provider will want to make it work. However, just like in a marriage, there is give and take. While shortcomings can be forgiven, divorce or separation, is always a possibility.

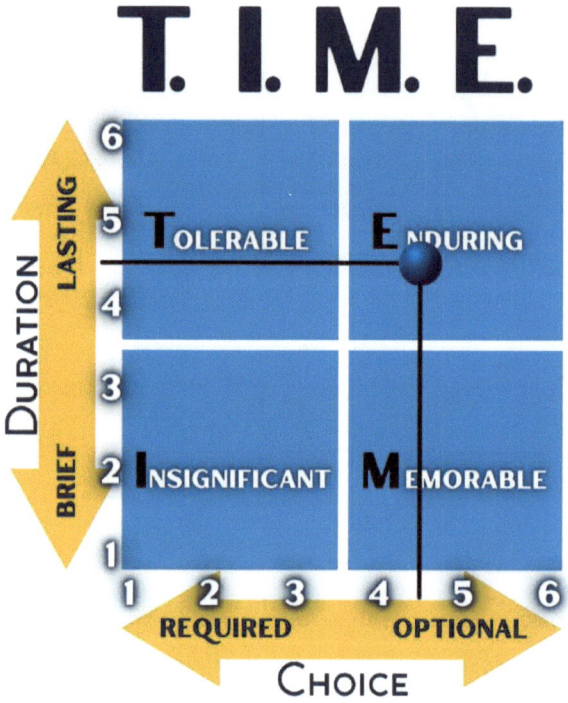

Remember that any quadrant can be good or bad and carries its own pros and cons. Therefore, if you want to keep your customers you need to ensure you use the Customer Hierarchy of Needs Strategy. All relationships require investment. So, creating a plan for loyalty is a good idea. However, understanding your level of investment will help insure you don't give away the farm. If you overinvest, just know you will likely never see a return on that money.

RELATIONSHIP CORRELATION MODEL (RCM)

Once you establish they type of relationship you have with your customers you can move on to journey mapping the customer phases with your company. This model explains each of the relationship phases comparing the phase of the personal and the business relationship. Not every phase will be part of every relationship type. As an example, A toll booth operator does not need to be concerned with attracting customers. There is only one operator, that operator is well known, and the customers circumstances will drive them toward the purchase. Pun intended.

RELATIONSHIP CORRELATION

PERSONAL   BUSINESS

ATTRACTION=MARKETING

COURTSHIP=CONSUMER RESEARCH

COMMITMENT=PURCHASE

TRIAL & ERROR=SERVICE/PRODUCT FAILURE

MAKE AMENDS=SERVICE RECOVERY

FORK IN THE ROAD

RECOMMIT OR SEPARATE=PROMOTER OR DETRACTOR

ANOTHER SUITOR

The next few sections walk you through each of the phases in the RCM. I will also go over some Do's and Don'ts for each of these. Again, these are common relationship characteristics, so feel free to make your own and add them in. This is an instinctual and living theory. You will come up with your own that fit just as easily for your

The Human Customer Experience

company or industry. The important take away is to understand the phase you are in with your customer.

PERSONAL RELATIONSHIP CYCLE

OTHER SUITORS

RECOMMITMENT

FORK IN THE ROAD

MAKE IT RIGHT

TRIAL & ERROR

COMMITMENT

COURTSHIP

ATTRACTION

SEPERATION

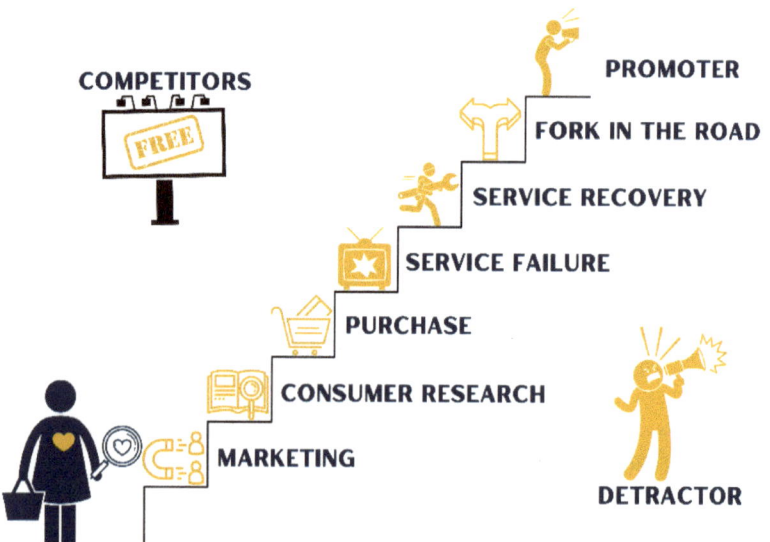

BUSINESS RELATIONSHIP CYCLE

COMPETITORS

FREE

PROMOTER

FORK IN THE ROAD

SERVICE RECOVERY

SERVICE FAILURE

PURCHASE

CONSUMER RESEARCH

MARKETING

DETRACTOR

ATTRACTION/MARKETING

If you are looking to find a partner, you put a little lipstick on, wear your best dress, and go out to be seen. Your business has to do the same. The important thing is to be real. Don't waste money advertising to be something you are not. Don't worry about appealing to everyone; there will be an entire school of fish that aren't interested in what you are selling. It's okay because there are other fish that are looking especially for you.

What makes this phase GREAT! You are always at your best. No worries of bed head or morning breathe. You get to put your best foot forward every time your customer interacts with your brand.

DO'S AND DON'TS:

DO: Enhance your best features.

Use branding and logos to create recognition. Focus on the features of your P/S (Product or service) and how they help the customer.

DON'T: Fake-it.

Avoid making claims that are untrue simply because it is a choice your competitor has or something the customer wants. They will figure out soon enough you were not being honest and the hurdle for recovery is too high to jump.

DO: Get out there.

Your perfect customer will not walk through your front door if they don't have your address; nor would your soul mate find you if you aren't out looking. Not advertising is the kiss of death for any company or spinster.

DO: Know your market

Find how your customer shops and spend wisely on advertising. Like they say, if you want to marry a millionaire go where millionaires spend time together. Understand why they buy, when, where, how, and who is most likely to purchase and target them. This is a time when it is okay to stereotype.

DO: Market to Your customers.

When you know your customers, you can market to them directly. If your product appeals to an urban environment use billboard, if it appeals to suburban's take out an ad in the newspaper, and if it appeals to the rural areas get an ad in a local publication. You wouldn't advertise a junked out car at a country club any more than you would market a new tattoo shop to the PTA. And of course, find the social

The Human Customer Experience

media platform that most appeals to your target demo rather than the one you are most familiar with.

DON'T: Talk about your competition.

You need to understand you aren't the only game in town. You also need to know how you stack up against the competition. But the last thing you should do is show your hand to your customers. Customers may not be aware of your competition or how much better they are. Don't help them learn through your hard earned advertising budget. Studies have also shown that customers don't appreciate it and it makes your company appear desperate and undesirable. No one wants that, not you and certainly not your customer.

Add your own Do's and Don'ts For ATTRACTION/MARKETING

COURTSHIP/CONSUMER RESEARCH

You are laying the foundation of your relationship. This is when you learn about on another to see if you are a good fit. It is critical you be honest and up front. Be sure you don't sell yourself short or they may move on to someone else. Strive for a balance of available and hard to get.

What makes this phase GREAT! You are much more forgiving of mistakes because of the natural high of something new and exciting. You tend to overlook flaws. This is when we are eager to please and are the most forgiving.

DO'S AND DON'TS:

DO: Set the groundwork for the future.

Be clear about what you are going to offer and what you won't. If you are going to send flowers every week forever, then it's okay to let them know. But if it is only for six months, be very clear up front that is what is happening. And know that after six months there could still be hurt feeling when it ends. Humans are creatures of habit, and we get used to things the way they are. When you change what the customer is used to, you change how valuable the belief is of what they are receiving. Most importantly, you have to be prepared to follow through. If not, avoid setting up the expectation. Don't offer unlimited data for the first few months and then change your mind and expect us not to be upset and possibly even leave. You broke a promise, so might we.

DON'T: Bluff.

This one should be obvious, but we sometimes think we can get away with something. Even if you do, you have created a relationship built on dishonesty and it is doomed. If you can't offer what the customer needs, then say so. You will gain much more respect.

DO: Know what you're worth.

In this phase you are setting the value of your product. Discounting your P/S to encourage a purchase is only good in the short term. Too long and you change what you are worth in the customers' mind.

DO: Be hard to get. (But, don't play hard to get)

There is a difference between being in high demand or exclusive and trying to convince someone you are. It is okay to have a long waiting list or be part of a private club. In fact, these things will raise your perceived value in the customer's mind. However, if you aren't really as busy or in demand as you express to be when they figure it out it will start to erode very valuable trust. Being too eager will also

The Human Customer Experience

make a customer wonder if you are the right choice. Why would they want your P/S if no one else does?

DON'T: Fork it up before it starts.

At the end of a relationship, you come to a fork in the road. Sometimes that end comes before it ever starts. If you do not meet expectations, don't deliver on a promise, or even aren't attractive enough because someone better came along, you will be left behind. Some things you can't control like changing your product offering for just one person, but other things like discovering their needs and ensuring you deliver are within your control.

Add your own Do's and Don'ts for COURTSHIP/CONSUMER RESEARCH

COMMITMENT/PURCHASE

This is what you have been working toward; the process should be seamless and simple. Understand that your partner had "many fish in the sea" and they still chose you. Show your customer's appreciation by saying thank you for the little things.

What makes this phase GREAT! This is the real deal. You can be comfortable that this relationship is happening. Enjoy the positives that come with being committed to each other.

DO'S AND DON'TS:

DO: Encourage commitment

The decision has been made, they went with YOU! Now you need to remind your customer why they made that decision and that it was the right one. This is especially true with larger purchases where buyer's remorse can set in. The last thing you need is uneasiness when you are just getting started.

DON'T: Get too comfortable

If the deposit is made, the plan is set the money is exchanged; you may tend to slack off. You may not care as much now as you did before. They are here; they are yours. What is there to worry about? EVERYTHING. Now is the hard part. You actually have to deliver on what you promised. On top of that, things could fall apart. There is always a chance of divorce. You also want to keep your customer happy, so they don't start looking for a better deal.

DO: Value the commitment

A little appreciation can go a long way. I once received an email from a company I purchased from online. They just wanted to make sure the delivery arrived. I was so excited about it that I immediately went on social media and complimented them as well as posting a link to their store. It doesn't have to be big; it just needs to be genuine. It is always a human who makes the purchase.

DON'T: Take each other for granted

If you have a customer who always pays on time, sometimes even in advance. Make sure they know you appreciate it. When the time comes to tighten the purse, you will have a better chance of it continuing. The little things you do for each other to keep one another happy are important.

DO: Appreciate each other's little gestures.

With something as simple as saying thank you for answering a question over email, you can make all the difference. You are setting up a foundation on which you will build your relationship and

The Human Customer Experience

expectations. A good customer interaction can outweigh a bad one, especially if they have experienced several great interactions over time.

Add your own Do's and Don'ts for COMMITMENT/PURCHASE

TRIAL AND ERROR/SERVICE FAILURE

Relationships have issues. Get in front of the issue when you can. When you can't, understand it is a big deal to the customer; even if it is an everyday occurrence to you. Never assume your customer is lying, as nothing destroys trust faster. Trust and communication are critical to any lasting relationship, listen to their side and assume good intent.

What makes this phase GREAT! As much as this phase can damage the relationship, it can also create an even stronger bond. Also, these are likely to be, little things, irritations, nuisances, not the big deals that end relationships.

DO'S AND DON'TS:

DO: Acknowledge Reality

Poorly designed features or parts of the P/S that do not work in the best way will soon irritate your customer. Understanding these pieces and creating a solution is a proactive path. However, if the customer is the one to bring these to your attention accept them as true even if only in their belief. Theirs is the only one that matters. This is no time for ego or fighting your customer's reality.

DON'T: Take it lightly

Just because a commitment was made doesn't mean it is an unbreakable bond. Dismissing a customer's concern at this stage will only set you up for a more difficult road in the future. Always take a complaint seriously and do your best to turn it around. It is a delicate balance.

DO: Understand both sides of the story.

Everyone has a perspective and then there is the truth. Understand where your customer is coming from before saying no, or yes for that matter. The customer isn't always right, but when they are, make sure your acknowledge it and sometimes, even when they aren't, it is better to be happy than it is to be right.

DON'T: Say something you'll regret

Unless you are really ready for divorce, then don't let it get that far. Don't threaten something you are not willing to follow through on. It makes you seem disingenuous and whinny. Remember you can't take back things you say in the heat of the moment. With your spouse or your customer, they will remember how you treat them.

Add your own Do's and Don'ts for

The Human Customer Experience
TRIAL AND ERROR/SERVICE FAILURE

MAKING IT RIGHT/SERVICE RECOVERY

Depending on how well you handle these first issues, you could either strengthen your relationship, or set it down a doomed path. This is a time to build trust. Is there anything worse than having the same issue over, and over, and over, and... well you get the idea. Fix it right the first time.

What makes this phase GREAT! Fixing issues opens hearts. And everyone knows the best time to ask for something you really want, like a motorcycle, is right after you have fully buttered up your spouse. It's a great opportunity to try for a new sale, in the right situations.

DO'S AND DON'TS:

DO: Recover well.

Good recovery is vital. Depending on how well you handle these first issues, you could either strengthen your relationship, or set it down a doomed path. This is a time to build trust or blow it away. Choose carefully, choose happy, over right.

DON'T: Get in a power struggle.

In this phase of the relationship, reality is setting in. The customers are coming to terms with, "you get what you pay for." While not all the discoveries are going to be bright and shiny, they are real. When that happens, it can be easy for our ego's to get in the mix and try to make think or feel a certain way. Be willing to change, be willing to stand your ground, and understand when each should happen.

DON'T: Hide the truth.

If you can't fix the problem, be honest. If your spouse is a cheat, and will always be a cheat, wouldn't you rather know earlier? Don't make your customer wait to figure it out on their own. It will cause resentment. Who knows, they may not mind your faults if you are open and honest about them.

DO: Fix it right the first time.

Is there anything worse than having the same issue over and over? At some point your customer will say enough is enough. Fix it right the first time. When something comes up, make sure you fully understand the issue and resolve it. This is where your proactive planning in problem solving and creating post incident reviews really help.

Add your own Do's and Don'ts for

The Human Customer Experience

MAKING IT RIGHT/SERVICE RECOVERY

FORK IN THE ROAD

When trial and error is over and service recovery isn't working anymore, there is a decision to be made. To be or not to be? At this point, when you decide to stay, you are choosing with full knowledge of what they look like in the morning, bad breath and all. This phase is really about the moment when a decision needs to made and less about what happens next.

What makes this phase GREAT! There is no illusion. You have faltered and you have recovered, likely many times. If you choose to stay, the issues that plagued you before will not be as dramatic. You can't be blindsided again, you already know how it is.

DO'S AND DON'TS:

DON'T: Let go without a fight!

If you want to keep the relationship you will have to fight. You will have to be willing to change and accommodate, if not, it is likely the relationship will not last. The more of an investment you have made to get the customer as well as the difficulty in replacing them will determine how hard you need to fight to keep them.

DO: Understand that it takes two.

A relationship will not last without both parties trying. You can't fix it alone. If they aren't in it, there is a time when you need to let go. The good news is that if your customer is letting you know there is a problem, they are still invested in the relationship.

DON'T: Ignore, neglect, or withdraw.

If you want this thing to work, you have to get in there and do the hard work. Sitting back and waiting on someone else to decide will not work. Passiveness will kill the relationship. You have to be willing to hear what they are saying and take if serious enough to do something about it.

DO: Let go when the time is right!

Often the healthiest thing you can do is step back and understand that you are not meant for each other. Evaluate and take action. When a customer costs too much to keep or can never be happy even with your best, you may need to let them go. It's okay; relationships are a two way street.

The Human Customer Experience

**Add your own Do's and Don'ts for
FORK IN THE ROAD**

RECONCILIATION OR SEPARATION/
PROMOTER OR DETRACTOR

This is the final stage in most relationships, otherwise referred to as divorce. Some relationships will continue in which case it is reconciliation. But either way, there is a lot of water under the bridge. If you decide to go your separate ways, it can be just as emotionally involved as a bitter divorce. Especially if you make divorce difficult, name calling, failing to deliver as promised, or drawing out the break up. There is a right way to break up and wrong way, and the same is true with customers. After all, many times the company would be open to the customer returning so getting it right is even more critical.

What makes this phase GREAT! If you do decide to stay the commitment is stronger, expectations are less idealistic and closer to reality. You have been through a lot. You can't take this thing for granted. For customers, this is anyone who is with you longer than the typical life cycle.

DO'S AND DON'TS:

DO: Appreciate it for what it is.

You had a good run. Regardless of if it is continuing or ending, ensure that you are grateful for what was. It taught you lessons you can apply to all areas. There is something about this relationship that has been wonderful. Be sure to keep those things in mind.

DO: Learn from your mistakes.

Because you were taught lessons, good and bad, ensure that you take those lessons and apply them. Use that knowledge in all parts of your business to make needed improvement and every experience that comes next, even that much better for everyone.

DON'T: Close the door.

Sometimes a relationship that has ended will want to come back together. Making divorce difficult will only create animosity and solidify your customers' decision to leave. If you make it easy and show appreciation you will be taking the first step toward opening that door again. If you are choosing to continue the relationship it is important not to go on acting like nothing happened. Be open and willing to discuss the issue so you can avoid getting to this point again.

DON'T: Bring others into it.

In a personal relationship, this is all about the kids, in-laws and mutual friends. In business relationships this is about other customers, employees, and competitors. It is important not to add drama or involve

The Human Customer Experience

other people in the issues between you and your customer; there just isn't a good way for that to end.

Add your own Do's and Don'ts for
RECONCILIATION OR SEPARATION/
PROMOTER OR DETRACTOR

ANOTHER SUITOR

Your customer is a great catch. Half the battle is creating a heart that has no need to wonder. You should never forget that. You worked hard at one time, spent money, and made investments to get them. Even when they are shopping other competitors can find their way in. It is important to know and understand your competition so you can either plan a defensive strategy or at least counteract their claims of superiority.

What makes this phase GREAT! Nothing, it isn't a phase, and it isn't great. The only positive that could come from this part is that the other suitor could reaffirm how perfect you are. Are you willing to take that chance?

DO'S AND DON'TS:

DO: Acknowledge reality.

You are not the only one who will find your customer attractive. They have great qualities, not the least of which is a desire for what you sell and the means to buy it.

DON'T: Ignore the warning signs.

Warning signs are little things like spending less time with you, not as interested in what you have to say, and bigger things like saying, "I think we need to see other people."

DO: Be confident.

Keep your confidence about what a great catch you are; they chose you once. Looking weak or undesirable is not the way to keep someone interested. Remind your customers of your great features as often as you can.

DON'T: Waste a second on the competition.

Don't waste your time on the competition; you may enlighten them to features or benefits of the "other guy" they didn't even know about. Focus on your products. If you need to make sure your customers know you are better talk about that feature that the other can't touch, just don't mention him when you do.

DO: value what you have.

No relationship is 100 percent impenetrable to competitors. So do your best every day to remind them you value them, and you have exactly what they need.

Add your own Do's and Don'ts for

The Human Customer Experience

ANOTHER SUITOR

THE CUSTOMER RELATIONSHIP MODEL

To know how you should invest in your customer experience, you need to map your typical customer experience. This doesn't have to be large and in depth, although you should always have a working understanding of the typical customer path. You should also figure out where your industry falls on the DCM. Once you know their place, you can apply the RCM to the different phases. Then you can determine how to integrate the do's and don'ts into each phase. This will help you understand when (and if) you will get return on your investment as you implement customer relationship strategies. It will also help you understand if you have opportunities to lengthen your current life cycle and improve the life-time value of your customer.

If you haven't done a customer journey map before for your business, now is the time. It will help facilitate the final step. A customer journey map details the most likely path a customer travels with your company. There are always one-off situations and thus do not need to be included on the journey map. This is a look at the typical customer's path from "birth to death." This may also be called the customers life cycle.

For each phase or your customers journey you should be able to answer three questions:

- What is your current state for each of these phases,
- Is your current state working, and
- If not, what should it look like?

Use the earlier Do/Don't descriptions as a guide when figuring out what your phase looks like or should look like. Many times, without knowing it a company will set themselves up for failure by creating a process that is counterintuitive to what a human is expecting from the relationship. Even the best intentions can be thrown over by an emotional heart.

The Human Customer Experience

It is also important to keep in mind which quadrant your industry falls in. Those in the Insignificant quadrant, for example, are not needed, nor do they benefit from added investment in relationship marketing. If your company lives in the Tolerable quadrant, on the other hand, you may not benefit from added investment, but it is expected in order to maintain good relations and make solving customer issues easier. For the Memorable quadrant, investment isn't expected, but it is freely given as a way to foster an open door for future purchases. And in the Enduring quadrant, investment is expected, needed, and reciprocated.

Beyond the journey map, how can you know you are delivering on the needs of your customer? That is where our third and final concept comes in to play.

KEY TO SUCCESS

Regardless of your path, cycle, or place, you have an obligation and a duty to deliver to the customer as promised. There is a difference between delivering and DELIVERING. The least expensive way to get more customers and the most loyal customers is to create positive, emotional, unexpected experiences that will travel through word of mouth from your satisfied customers. The most basic truth for a successful delivery is to simply be human. Maslow outlined for us what it means to be human and how to satisfy our needs with his hierarchy chart. This model has been adapted to align with customer needs.

CUSTOMER'S HIERARCHY OF NEEDS

Delivering experiences that leave a lasting impression follow the basic hierarchy of needs that Maslow outlined for human needs. There are five levels of needs, one dependent on the other. It starts with having your product or service in working order, after all if your P/S isn't even working or deliverable, you can't meet the basic need of the customer. There is no amount of customer service, empathy, or "making it right" that can make up for a failed P/S. This is the starting point, at the bottom of the pyramid. When you hit this milestone, you get to move up, one by one. In summary: "**Make your customers lives better by showing them respect with a genuine interest; always delivering as promised and in working order.**"

So, let's find out a little more about each level of this new pyramid and how you can use it to ensure you have a fully developed business model to wow and delight your customers. Creating customers who want to come to back for more and tell are their friends and family about you in the meantime.

CUSTOMER'S HIERARCHY OF NEEDS

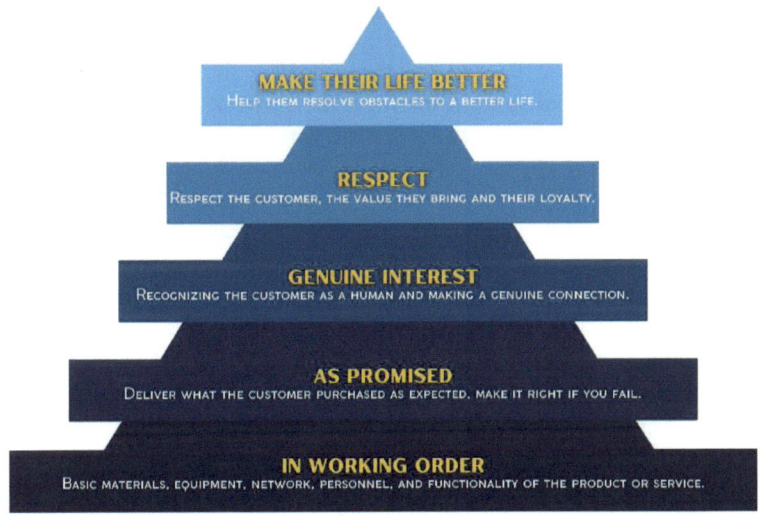

IN WORKING ORDER

Before you can satisfy any other need, you must make sure your product or service works. You have to fulfill the basic requirements of material, equipment, infrastructure, personnel, and ensure it functions. You can't hope to meet the other factors of the customers' expectations and needs if your product or service is broken. You don't even get off the ground. You can't pass go. And you most certainly can't collect $200.

AS PROMISED

Once the material basics of the product or service have delivered and you ensure they are getting what they paid for. Next you make sure it is delivered in the way it was promised, or how the customer is expecting. If there are service failures or delivery interruptions, they need to be addressed and made right. Unfortunately, this is where some businesses think the customer's needs end when it comes to experience, service, and relationships. But ask yourself this, if you only talked to your spouse when there was a broken appliance or you account was overdrawn, would you enjoy and appreciate your relationship? This is still just the beginning of the relationship.

GENUINE INTEREST

Next, you need to make a genuine connection with the customer. This is where the real customer service starts. We recognize the individual person and connect to them. Over the phone or in person, you have a real conversation, not a scripted one. Even better if you have a CRM system that can track this information and allows you to recall these little details like their dogs' names, or their preferred way they order their drink. Imagine going to the same coffee shop every day for 6 months. You order the same drink from the same 2-3 people and even after 6 months none of them seem to even remember your face, let alone your order or any details about you. Wouldn't that make you feel incredibly unseen and unappreciated. How much loyalty would you have to that shop if someone opened closer to your home or office?

RESPECT

Once you connect to your customer, you can start showing them you respect them. You respect the fact their business is what keeps your doors open and you understand even though they have other choices, likely more than one, they have chosen you. You respect their time, their needs, and work to ensure you don't fail to live up to their expectations. But you can't just jump here. You have to jump through the hurdles of the other steps. If you can't deliver on what your customer purchased, if you can't deliver it as promised, if you can't show them, you see them, they aren't going to hear you when you try to make this connection. It will feel disingenuous and fake. It will have the opposite impact. You will make them feel like you are checking a box or worse that you don't respect them at all.

MAKE THEIR LIFE BETTER

If you have made it through all the other levels, the customer only at this point allow you to make this leap as well. Here you have established trust; you have fulfilled the basic requirements and shown the customer you do have their best interest in mind. So, when you launch a new feature or option, they don't think you are telling them just get another dollar, they understand that you also want to help them improve their life. Your motives are no longer questioned, they are accepted as true and reasonable. You can work with them to bring more of your brand into their life and solve their personal obstacles. If you are a coach who offers a valuable educational seminar, one aspect of your business is connecting them to others who can help them as well. This is something you do to build them up. You might get a kick back for this, you might not. Either way, you won't be allowed "in" if you can't first deliver on the other four. Your motives will be questioned.

CONCLUSION: BEING HUMAN

In the moment, if you don't remember anything else from this process or these models, just remember this. You already have all the tools you need to create amazing customer experiences. All you have to do is lean in and BE HUMAN. Find or create a moment of human connection. Be kind, honest, and trustworthy. Be genuine and find ways to add value to your customers' life, without any other agenda than helping them. With or without your product. Customers will <u>always</u> respond to a true human connection.

Trust your gut, because when we get out of the way, our instinct will guide us. What feels right? Does the decision you are making about your customer or the experience you are giving them make you feel good or bad? Not because your boss said so, not because your coworker did the same thing, not because you saw your competitors do it. What feels right to you?

There are a hundred ways to conduct a blind study, do field research, test marketing for promotional buy in, and you should do all of that. But in the moment, when you are face to face with the customer, and when you are deciding to say yes or no, to place a one week welcome call or a send a two week promotional up sell mailer, what does your gut say is the right answer. What kind of relationship do you have, where are you in the process, and how much trust have you built?

Now, get going! Build your map. Plan your journey. **Love your Customer.**

Thank you for reading The Human Customer Experience and the Not-So-Secret Formula. Hopefully you will be able to incorporate this in your business.

If you would like a workbook to complete for your business just scan the QR code on the next and follow the instructions. I will sent you a free PDF you can you print off and use.

Thank you again for your purchase and support of indie this Author!

The Human Customer Experience

If you enjoyed this book please leave a review on Amazon, Good Reads, Google, or you preferred book review platform. Your review helps ensure others find this book as well. For indie authors, you are our only way of life! Thank you so much for your support!

This QR code will take you directly to Amazon to review this book.

Please go to DesireeMPalmer.com to check out Desiree's other work. To sign up for her newsletter go to Satori.pub

When you sign up, you will receive free downloadable PDF worksheet based on this publication to use with your business. Just say which publication you purchased when signing up!

This QR code will take you directly to Satori.Pub to sign up for the newsletter and request your PDF.

Check out these other titles by Desiree:
Energy Evolution
My Evolution: Energy Evolution Journal
Lifestyle Plan: Mind body Soul
Lifestyle Plan: Success Journal